Echoes of Epiphany

OrangeBooks Publication

1st Floor, Rajhans Arcade, Mall Road, Kohka, Bhilai, Chhattisgarh 490020
Website: **www.orangebooks.in**

First Edition, 2025

ISBN: 978-93-6554-418-3

Price: Rs. 175.00

Printed in India

Echoes of Epiphany

Arnab Bhowmick

OrangeBooks Publication
www.orangebooks.in

About The Author

Arnab Bhowmick is an award-winning poet and an emerging voice in contemporary poetry, recognised for his profound emotional depth and lyrical clarity. In 2024, he received the 21st Century Emily Dickinson Award for his debut poetry collection, Verses of the Healing Soul. This work touched hearts across generations with its quiet wisdom and soulful resonance.

Driven by an unwavering devotion to the written word, Arnab weaves his verses from threads of realism, introspection, and timeless beauty. His poetry reflects a deep reverence for nature, emotion, and the human spirit, echoing the influences of literary greats like John Keats and William Wordsworth. Much like them, he seeks to transform the ordinary into the extraordinary through the power of language.

As an aspiring novelist as well, Arnab continues to explore the vast landscape of human experience, encouraging readers not only to look outward but to journey inward.

Connect with him on

Instagram:@quill_whispers

Dedication

To the young dreamers, students, professionals, and seekers who are constantly moving forward in pursuit of success, this book is a reminder. A reminder to slow down, to observe life closely, and to truly experience its essence.

May you never be too busy to sit with your parents, to enjoy a moment of quiet joy, or to extend kindness to those in need. In the race for achievement, may you not forget what it means to be human, to care, to respect, to protect, especially the women around you.

And above all, may you always carry gratitude in your heart for this life, for its lessons, and for the light that still shines, even on the hardest days.

***Echoes of Epiphany* is dedicated to you.**

Acknowledgement

First and foremost, I extend my deepest gratitude to God, whose boundless grace and guidance have illuminated my path and made this journey possible. Your Divine wisdom has been my strength and inspiration.

To my parents, thank you for your unwavering support and boundless love. Your encouragement and sacrifices have shaped me into who I am today. I am forever grateful for your belief in me.

To my dear sister, your constant presence and encouragement have been a source of joy and motivation. Your understanding and support have been invaluable to me.

To my beloved wife, whose love and companionship have been my greatest treasure. Thank you for your patience, understanding, and for standing by my side through every challenge. Your belief in me has been a guiding light.

To the exceptionally talented illustrators, Somshukla Adhya and Ranit Paul, whose artistry brought the pages of this book to life. The evocative and meaningful sketches throughout would not have been possible without your creative vision and dedication.

Finally, my heartfelt thanks to the publisher, whose belief in this work and professional expertise have made this publication a reality. Your dedication and support have been truly remarkable.

With gratitude and love,

~ Arnab Bhowmick

Preface

Some books are written.

This one... descended.

Each poem in *Echoes of Epiphany* arrived like a breath from beyond, a sacred whisper carried through time, asking not to be authored but revealed. These are not just verses; they are visions. Not reflections of the world as we see it, but glimpses of the world as it *truly* is through a divine kaleidoscope where light fractures into meaning, and shadows sing their secrets.

This collection is my quiet rebellion against the ordinary. It urges you, dear reader, to peel back the veil and look beyond the dull edges of daily life. To see the truth behind ageing parents' eyes... the slow fading of heroes... the silent collapse of things we thought were certain and eternal.

These poems walk through the ruins of illusion and speak to a reality where our fragility is holy. Where the human spirit trembles before forces vast, unseen, and divine. Where Dracula feed not from fables, but from the marrow of modernity through greed, despair, and a hunger that wears a thousand masks.

You can find the raw hymn of existence jagged, beautiful, and humbling. A song sung not by me, but through me. I am merely the pen. The voice belongs to the infinite.

Echoes of Epiphany is not a book to be understood. It is to be *felt*. Let the words break you open. Let them flood your heart with both darkness and light. Let them remind you that we are, all of us, dust on the breath of something divine.

This collection is an offering. A bow. A humble surrender to the great power that governs all things. Through these poems, I invite you not to understand, but to feel. Not to search for meaning, but to stand still before the mystery and get lost in the *echoes of your epiphanies*.

Contents

A Kaleidoscope Unseen

Step out, escape the shadows where the world is framed,
Beyond the glassy screens and wires, untamed.
A thousand faces, trapped in pixels, cold and bright
Come, glimpse the world through a different light.

The rain, it falls, a tender kiss from skies unspoken,
A wind that whispers secrets, soft but broken.
Pause and breathe; let the stillness call your name,
For in the race of time, what do you truly claim?

You toil each day beneath a flickering glow,
Numbers and letters in a ceaseless flow.
A blue-collared soul in a polished guise,
Trapped in the grind that blinds our eyes.

But look! The trees sway with ancient grace,
Their roots dig deep in the earth's embrace.
The laughter of kin, the warmth of the hearth
Are treasures far richer than all you're worth.

Do not squander time in the chase for more,
For death waits patiently behind every door.
Grudges are burdens too heavy to bear,
And love, though fleeting, is always there.

So work with vigour, but do not miss
The joy of the moment, the simple bliss.
For life is brief, like a dream half-spun,
Live fully, before the day is done.

You Are My Life Jacket

I care not for the cliffs,
Nor the wild depths of the sea,
For you are the shelter that holds me,
My refuge in the storm,
My anchor beneath the tempest sky.

No chains can bind me,
No winds can sway me
For I am free,
Untouched, unbroken, as long as you stand with me,
A fortress in the tide.

In my youth, I wandered through dreams,
Of distant lands that never came.
I spun fables, believing in them,
And yet, I found you there
A miracle, whispered by the universe,
Unfolding the stars at my feet.

Together, we share the golden dusk,
The breath of sunsets we can call our own,
And the maps of foreign shores
We trace with fingers intertwined.

No horizon frightens me now,
For you are my constant,
My life jacket
In the ocean of all I have yet to be.

A Warning To The Tomb Raiders

Disturb not the earth where we now sleep,
For in life, peace was but a fleeting dream.
Now, in silence, we seek the stillness we were denied.

No treasure lies beneath, no spoil for the thief's grasp.
Tread lightly, for the soil may turn against you,
And soon you may find yourself among us.

When the night wind stirs and the chill touches your skin, know we are near,
Watching your every move unseen, unheard.
Though we bow to the earth, let not our silence be mistaken for mercy.

Treat us with care or leave us undisturbed,
For cruelty shall find no welcome here.

Do not crush the flowers our loved ones left behind,
For they mourn in silence, grieving what was lost.
We have set our gaze upon a distant horizon,
Bound by penance unfulfilled and mysteries yet to unfold.

Let us rest in peace, undisturbed
For in life, peace was but a shore we could never reach.

Ode To The Omnipotent: A Confrontation With Ego

What is this reckless courage that bids me, bold,
To pen Your name yet in pride, so uncontrolled?
Still, here I stand, with trembling heart and hand,
Seeking to trace the contours of Your command.

We, self-proclaimed as kings, with pride in bloom,
Believe our trials, their bitter depths, consume
Our wisdom shapes us into fools forlorn,
As if the crucible of pain had not been borne
By You, the sculptor of our fleeting grace,
Who moulds our fates in silence, soft and base.

It is Your breath that gives our names their spark;
Through ink and thought, You've left Your sacred mark.
Yet here we stand, in insolence aglow,
Blind to the seeds You planted long ago.

Emotions, tempest-tossed, illusions wild
Spun from Your hand, the Weaver reconciled.
Still, we rise, as if on wings of air,
Claiming victories that were never ours to bear.
In pride, we bask, as if we alone had sown
The laurels that, by Your grace, have grown.

What if, at last, we stood before Your face,
In silence deep, within Your holy space?
Would we not fall hearts barren, humbled low,
Surrendering the pride we did not know?
Our souls would weep for all we'd done amiss,
Repenting sins cloaked in the fog of bliss.

Bowed heads would break beneath the weight of shame,
As we remember, through tears, our self-made claim.
And should Your mercy touch us in that hour,
Tears would fall from the heart's true power.

In that moment, all we'd truly know
Is that how little we sowed, and how much we owe?
For in Your grace, our hearts would find their home,
And in surrender, we'd cease to roam.

Yet, after the tears, what shall remain
But gratitude, unspoken, free from pain?
A quiet awe, a deep and still refrain
That we, though unworthy, were not left in vain.

For in Your mercy, boundless as the sky,
We learn, at last, to lift our hearts on high
Not to claim, but to thank, for all we are,
A fleeting spark, yet bright beneath Your star.

The Passage Of Time: A Requiem For Parents

Time, a river, flowing swift and sure,
It carries all that we love, with a gentle blur.

Our parents, once towering, now bow beneath
The weight of years, and sickness' s cruel wreath.
The fear, like shadows, stretches inch by inch,
As they wither, slow, and our hearts pinch.
In pursuit of dreams, we drift far away,
Chasing something, I know not what to say.
What lies ahead, unknown, elusive, cold,
As they grow frail and the world grows old.

Once, their voices rang with strength, with pride,
Guiding us through life, with wisdom wide.
Now we see them, uncertain, hands that shake,
Eyes that flicker, like a flame about to break.
The reins are handed, trembling, to our grasp,
And with it, the weight of every task.
Their nerves, like tough strings, quiver in their face
And we, their children, tremble in their place.
A shock, a burden, how can we repay
The love they gave, the price they did not weigh?
But thanks to God, to them, to every care,
I stand, their strength returned in prayer.

Every holiday, when we return,
Their eyes, like lanterns, eager to discern,
They listen to our words with patient grace,
Their hearts are alive, though time has left its trace.
Yet, how we falter, in haste to cut the thread,
Business calls, urgent whispers in our head.
We cannot stay, though their faces plead,
Our hearts are torn between love and worldly need.

But in that fleeting glance, I understand,
Time slips from our hands, like shifting sand.
Yet love remains, though worn, though strained,
A bond that distance cannot break or feign.
We are the children, now grown to hold
The hands of those who once, so brave and bold.

Caged In Silence

Oh, how inconsiderate to lock them in a room,
While you are away, their hours of gloom.

Return, and there they are, eyes full of glee,
Greeted with love, such entertainment, for thee!
But let me ask, dear friend, do you not see?
A pet's true purpose isn't to entertain thee.
Once, in darker times, man knew restraint,
In prisons cold, where food and rest did taint.

And now, with loving hands, you hold the key,
To cage the souls of those who roam so free.

You claim to love them - ah, what a jest!
A lover of pets? You ought to do your best.
For animals, too, feel sorrow and strain,
Their minds and bodies wear the same pain.
To tether them, to cage them all day long,
It is to make the heart of sanity go wrong.
So here's a thought, a gentle check, my friend,
Consider - what this love may truly send.
For animals, like us, seek joy and peace,
Not lives of endless hours, that never cease.

In Search Of Simpler Times

Let me speak of days lost in time,
When today's youth could scarcely climb.
A black-and-white world, one channel clear,
Doordarshan's glow, the crowd would cheer.
Green fields are rare, like whispers gone,
Mangoes stolen during a tempest's song.
Jamun, spiced with salt and fire,
A treat so simple, it can never tire.
Grandma's jars, a treasure trove,
Pickles were packed with love and wove.
When power cuts brought twilight's chill,
We'd gather 'round, hearts to still.
Before today's world, when we were young,
Films were cheap, but manners were sung.
Magicians' tricks, a wonder's grace,
Fairs were bright, a joyous space.
Small joys bloomed in songs and sound,
Radio whispers, gramophones round.
Now, these relics of joy we see,
Just antique toys for the rich, to be.
Summer holidays, a simple delight,
Vacations close, yet felt so bright.

Now, with bigger budgets, we roam far,
But the joy seems distant, like a fading star.
Minimalism, once our guiding creed,
Now lost in excess, the hunger for speed.
Salaries shrink, digits fall,
By month's end, we feel so small.
We long to surrender, to give in,
To parents' arms, where peace begins.
The weight of the world, too much to bear,
A wish for simpler days, a prayer.

Where Certainty Crumbles

In this world where silence roars, where certainty crumbles,
A refusal to acknowledge the heart shapes our steps.
We march with hands stained by actions undone,
Seeking peace in the heavens,
But finding only the echoes of war.

A thirst remains, unquenched,
Its need buried beneath layers of words,
As knowledge, half-learned, slips through our fingers,
A faint prayer attempting to fill the void,
While the world burns unnoticed.

We speak of love,
But hold the blade of conviction,
Its edge sharpened by false certainty.
We call it righteousness,
Yet in it lies blasphemous reverence,
A reverence that poisons while it sanctifies.

The urge to silence doubt,
To bury the truth we refuse to see,
Keeps us in a cage of our own making,
Where faith becomes both weapon and shield,
Each strike is a testament to our blindness.

In this world, where truth fractures,
We search through the ruins for meaning,
But all we find is the hollow echo
Of truths we've long forgotten.

Across the globe, education becomes a tool,
Half-formed, skewed by manipulation,
Feeding minds with half-truths,
And targeting the vulnerable.

Teenagers, hungry for answers,
Are, fed lies dressed as knowledge,
And institutions, once places of enlightenment,
Have become vessels of control.

Brainwashing, in plain sight,
Sways those who seek truth,
Turning their questions into mere whispers,
Lost beneath the weight of doctrine,
And the world continues to burn in silence.

In this world, where certainty crumbles,
We search for meaning in the ruins,
But find nothing more than the hollow echo
Of a God we've forgotten.

Where Draculas Reside

Have you wandered through the halls of Dracula's keep?
Where do they linger, unseen yet near?
Do not be fooled
No kind of Edward dwells here,
Nor shimmering illusions of a Swan lost in twilight.

In the shadowed cobweb of the city,
Mansions rise like grotesque monoliths,
Their gaping mouths exhaled the stench of rot.
Treasures, vile-born of decay, spill forth,
And charity dons a mask, thin and cracking.
Hospitals, false sanctuaries,
Do not heal, but seed death
A sickness of the soul, relentless and incurable.

This is no fever of the body,
But a malady that seeps,
A darkness that festers,
Unseen and unending,
Draping the city in its suffocating veil.

The nights descend, heavy and unfeeling,
As vampires drink deeply of their dark thirst.
Beware of the neighbour who shares your bread,
Beware of the silent stranger on the crowded bus.
Trust falters, crumbles,
In this God-abandoned expanse.
Statues of grief rise, cold and unyielding,
Echoing the cries of the silenced
The Cry of the Hour.

A victim's monument,
While shadows of guilt slither away,
Leaving a scapegoat to bear the weight.
Justice limps, grotesque and absurd,
A mockery of humanity's fragile hope.

Who are these monsters, these vampires among us?
They weave their webs within the hollow
cocoon of power,
Nestled in the government's embrace.
Hell does not burn beneath the earth;
It flickers and thrives within human hearts.

Here, Dracula resides.
Guard your safety, shield your dignity
For these are trifles in a world so skewed.
How do we meet the gaze of the victim?
Condolences drip like hollow rain,
Offered to parents robbed of justice.
Poor souls - they are left with tears.
May the door of the Lord swing open wide,
And grant them the justice this world denies.

The Cocoon Of Innocence

Keep to the warmth of the protective womb,
Do not venture forth,
For harshness reigns beyond the veil,
Where the cruel winds of life and death cloud the horizon.
The expectations of kin and strangers alike shall stifle your breath,
And the purity of your soul, once untainted, may wither.
Keep to the warmth of the shielded womb,
There is no safer place on earth or in heaven than a mother's womb.
Her nourishment flows, even when she is hungry,
Her love transcends the limits of earthly sustenance,
Such is the sacrifice of a mother, infinite and undying.
Keep to the warmth of the protective womb,
Outside, friends wear the guise of foes,
And from the cradle, judgments come, based on colour, caste, or creed.
Within, all dreams are real,
Within, all fairy tales are woven in truth and light.
Keep to the warmth of the caring womb,
The world beyond is a battleground
A space crammed with rivalry, struggle, and survival.

Thank the one who cradles you,
Thank the one who bears the agony of your growth,
Thank the one who attends to your every need,
Even in her sacrifice, she is steadfast.
Keep to the warmth of the holy womb,
For the outside world is a cruel expanse.
Here, you shall meet heartbreak,
Here, you shall learn to be moulded by time and trial,
You shall grow, but at the cost of a dead childhood,
A childhood buried beneath the weight of survival.

Whispers Through The Veil

If escape to a world of wonder were mine to claim,
I would seek the hidden door, the silent hinge,
Marching through the wardrobe to Narnia's breathless wilds,
Or stepping onto the platform that splits reality,
The nine and three-quarters passage is unseen by the unworthy.
Where is my portal, my secret gate?
A threshold so veiled, so small, it waits only for my hands to uncover it.
What lies beyond its mysterious arch?

Will it cast me back to the time before?
When the world was vast and the trees spoke In whispers,
When rivers ran free, their laughter unchained,
And the air sang pure songs to unburdened lungs,
When the mountains and fields came to us,
And we did not chase them for breath.

Or will it lead me to a realm of stories made flesh?
Where Cinderella's glass slipper finds its rightful foot,
And Snow White dances in the arms of love.
A place where Beauty sees through the monstrous mask,
And the Beast, no longer alone, finds solace in her gaze.
I am no Beauty, nor do I claim her grace
But if my destiny is to wear the guise of the Beast,
Let it be so, if a Beauty waits for me on the other side.

So here I stand, in quiet hope,
Yearning for the veil to part,
For the portal to reveal its secrets,
That I may step through,
To whatever world calls my name.

Where the Birthday Song Doesn't Reach

When a child succumbs to malnutrition,
When abandoned orphans are left to wither,
Or worse, when they are pawns of counterfeit pity
Who will light a candle for them?
Who will gently ask them to close their eyes,
To make a wish upon the fragile flame?
But wishes are distant stars to them,
Unreachable, unknowable.
Their only wish, if they dared to dream,
It is the hollow miracle of a full stomach.
Who will sing them a birthday song?

Winter gnaws at their bodies,
Wrapping them in frost where no warmth exists.
Their noses run, unchecked by caring hands,
Their tears fall, unnoticed by all but the wind.
Their cries are drowned beneath the roar of a passing train.
They stretch out their palms, not for themselves,
But for the shadows who own their suffering
Thugs who twist innocence into tools,
Who maim tiny limbs for a few coins,
Who barter little girls in the dark corridors of flesh.
Who will sing them a birthday song?

Hunger is their constant lullaby,
A gnawing hymn of emptiness,
The ghrelin consumes its own flame.
The railway platform, cloaked in dust and despair,
Vibrates with the passing trains,
Their bed is trembling beneath the weight
of the world.
They do not know cakes come in shades of hazelnut,
Or even of chocolate, vanilla's sweet cream.
They smile their brightest for the smallest gift, toffee,
Oblivious to the meaning of a Birthday song,
Or the joy it is meant to bring.
Will you sing them a birthday song?
Will you sing them a birthday song?

If Jack Were Alive

If only there had been another door of wood,
Another raft to hold the weight of love,
Our Jack might have lived,
A heart that burned too brightly for the cruel sea.
Yes, Jack of the Titanic,
The dreamer cast adrift,
If only Rose could have shared more space,
If only the abyss had not claimed its prize.

Titanic, the vessel of dreams and doom,
A cathedral of steel, adorned with mortal pride,
Her chandeliers gleamed like frozen stars,
Her halls whispered of splendour, fleeting as breath.

Rose might have wedded her wild-hearted muse,
The embrace of their outstretched arms,
An ode to life above the waves,
Would not have dissolved into an elegy of the deep.
If only the lifeboats had multiplied like hope,
If only the waters had spared more souls.

Imagine if Jack had never held that winning hand,
If fate's dice had fallen differently.
He would still haunt Parisian garrets,
Sketching beauty with a hand stained in
charcoal dreams.

Not even the loveliest of them would rival Rose,
Yet Jack would endure,
A phantom of passion, painting life from shadow.
Perhaps his name would echo through time,
Whispered alongside Picasso's,
A rival in the halls of eternity.

The Severed Kite

We begin with hands as careful as whispers,
Bending fragile paper to hold the breath of the sky.
A sail unfurled weightless, enduring
Ready to court the invisible power of the wind.

The tail trails, deliberate as footsteps,
Finding its rhythm, the quiet hymn of ascent.
Colours bleed and converge,
Fragments of thought,
Shaped not for Earth,
But for the endless dialogue of air.

When it rises, stretching its limbs toward light,
The string tightens, a tether to ambition.
It climbs higher, still higher
Outdaring the birds,
Whispering to them:
"See, I too am a creature unbound."

Others join, painted bodies of flight,
Some slender, some vast,
Each is a proclamation of desire.
And then the clash.
Strings bite and graze,
A sky-bound struggle to remain,

To claim the fleeting crown of solitude.
The hands below tremble with urgency,
Pilots in a silent war waged above.

One falls.
Severed, set free.
The wind embraces it wholly now,
Carrying it beyond ambition,
Into the raw ecstasy of release.
No one will speak its name,
Or recall its fleeting grandeur.
Forgotten, it spirals downward,
Landing not with triumph,
But quiet surrender.

A boy from the alleys finds it.
He has known kites only as distant dreams,
Bright specks beyond his reach.
He cannot ask for one.
He knows better than to ask.
But in his hands, this fallen fragment lives again.
He sees its tattered beauty,
And swears to restore its flight,
To lift it skyward once more,
To give it the dignity it deserves.

Oh, Architect Of Existence

You sculpt the stars, shield the frail, and shatter what
you shape.
This vessel is but your whisper, this mind, a flicker of
your thought.
Every motion, every breath woven by your will.

Yet, like a tempest in a teacup, the mighty
'I' rises, grasping illusions, claiming dominion
over dust.
I boast of victories, lament my losses, but from what
throne do I rule?
To whom do I offer my triumphs, and where do I cast
my blame?

I may move, yet destiny's quill has inked the path.
Unless I unshackle the 'I', surrender its stubborn chains,
the road turns rugged, the sky grows dark.

Yes, I may gather gold, drape myself in fleeting fame,
But whose hands shape this form? Whose breath fuels this soul?
A droplet belongs to the boundless sea,
A grain of sand to the endless dune, yet the
'I' swells, mistaking itself for a mountain,
Blind to the vastness of creation, deaf to the whisper of its Maker.

Oh Weaver of Worlds, break this brittle pride,
Ignite the lantern of truth!
Accept my surrender, steer my soul.
Let me be a ripple in your river, a servant to your song,
A hand that heals, a heart that helps, a light for the lost.

Ode To Mother Goddess

The air hums with farewell whispers
Rain bids adieu, and flowers rise in silent bloom.
The trees, draped in sorrow, shed their golden grief,
While the sky, robbed of its downy dreams,
Utters not a single cry.
The fields, unshaven, stretch toward the waning sun,
Wild sugarcane rustling like secrets in the wind.
A distant drumbeat calls our feet to move,
Remembering an old melody,
A song once cradled in love's embrace.
The air, thick with the spell of the devil's tree,
Wraps around us like unseen hands.
Are we enchanted? Or merely lost
In the dream of a season that knows no chains?
Autumn's enchantment winds around us,
Leading us forward in a silent procession.
Bare feet kiss the dew-drenched earth,
While the wind hums a ghostly hymn
A choir of withering leaves,
Whispering not of death, but return.
Beneath the hush of an autumn moon,
night jasmines fall soft, unshaken.

They rest in pale surrender,
A fleeting grace upon the ground,
Until careful hands lift them,
Weaving prayers into their fading perfume.
To the Mother, they yield,
Petals pressed in quiet devotion.
In Her light, the shadows tremble and break,
And the darkness, once certain,
dissolves into dawn.

To Mother With Love

Take me to those charming days past,
For I can't express how much of them I miss!
I remember being in her lap, last,
The feeling, oh Lord! was like eternal bliss.

I want to be a child again and be lost in that day,
Mother, oh mother take me in your lap again,
I recall the day when, with my mom, I used to stay,
God knows how I made myself refrain.

Far, far, how far away I've come?
Although I know her love will follow me,
She used to tell me how big I needed to become,
Decades have passed; don't know how much bigger I need to be?

Mother, you were very strict on me,
But 'twas your loving concern to make me perfect.
I now crave your strictness with agony,
Though happiness is everywhere, I can never forget.
Ma, I miss my favourite dishes in your hand,
And your tender nursing when I bled.
This pain of separation only we both can understand-
Can't forget how you chased me when I fled.
When sickness did me abound,

My mother's touch was always near.
I could feel her hugs all around,
And she kept at bay my fear.
Ma, do you miss my pranks and miss me as your boy?
Do you miss my voice and my cheer?
Do you still fondle my childhood toy?
And when you remember me, do you brush away a tear?

Lord, I can't pay my debt,
For all the love she has given.
But thou, love's lord, will not forget,
Her due reward and bless her on earth and in heaven.

Dwindling On Insecurities

Life quivers on uneasy ground,
Each turn was steeped in shadows of doubt.
Insecurity brews in the corners of our days,
A bitter drink poured by hands unseen

Industries rise and thrive on our fears,
Whispering of flaws we never knew we had.

The mirror, once a quiet companion,
now a cruel judge,
Measuring the lines upon our skin,
The silver in our hair,
The weight of our worth in fleeting reflections.
Hollywood smirks, Korea glows
Standards carved from glass,
Shattering the selves we used to love.

And the screen, ah, the screen,
A looking glass of misery.
Scroll once, and the world grows heavier:
A friend with deeper pockets,
A cousin in a grander home,
A neighbour's car gleaming like envy itself.
A lover too beautiful, a husband too rich, each pixel a thorn against the skin.

We chase, we compare, we crumble.
The race never ends, the prize never comes.
Surgeons sculpt dreams for a price too steep,
But no blade can carve away the weight of wanting.

Let the scrolling cease, let the noise hush
Dare to step away.
For in this chase, there is always one with more,
And peace lingers only
For those who dare to stop running.

Unfinished Goodbyes

The night is heavy with unspoken grief,
and the wind hums the names of the lost.
They walk the edge of bridges, listening to the river's call,
Or stand before the iron jaws of a coming train,
Or gaze at the silent noose that sways like a Whispering ghost.

Each story, a quiet funeral before the fall
a lover left behind, drowning in betrayal's cruel tide,
a farmer with hands calloused from toil, yet empty,
a student crushed beneath the weight of borrowed dreams,
a woman haunted by hands that once felt familiar,
a man eroded by words sharper than knives.

The world, indifferent, marches on,
while the burdened break beneath its weight.
And in their last breath, they wonder
was freedom ever meant to come this way?

Eremitism

The voices fade, one by one
Friends, once close, now echo in the distance.
Relatives, once warm, now ghosts at the threshold.
Even I have turned away,
Seeking the silence that once seemed absurd.

As a child, solitude was a punishment,
A thing to be chased away with laughter,
With the clatter of board games,
The interest in finishing new video games,
The endless chatter of cousins,
Laughter bubbled up like an untamed river.
Now, time splinters
Work life gnaws at the hours,
Traffic devours what remains,
And if marriage or a relationship anchors you,
Your soul bends to its demands.
Then come the children
Small hands pulling at the last threads of idleness.

You can't deny them company
Once you look at those innocent, demanding eyes.

Life moves quicker than ever,
Solitude is no longer exile but refuge,
Not born of bitterness but of necessity.
A quiet room, a closed door
Not to escape, but to return,
To listen to the hum of one's own thoughts.

Still, the office lingers in the skull,
It's rattle and din clinging to the bones.
A cold shower rinses the day, but not enough.
The past appears sweeter, nostalgia's soft whisper
But it is only a whisper.
The weight settles once more
The race continues.

And so, the voices drift further, further.
The ones I once held dear, now strangers.
And I, too, am a stranger to them.

Amber fields

Where once our home stood tall in fields of grain,
Where the sun turned crops to golden brown,
And harvest filled our eyes with wonder.

There we ran, free as the wind,
Through rivers of wheat,
As scarecrows watched as a silent audience.
Only to threaten in the darkness of night.

Love found me there, my first kiss,
A whisper in the furrows,
As summer's breath warmed the night,
And stars wove stories till sleep took hold.

Now the city hums where silence lay,
Chasing wealth and empty pride.
We lost real gold to dirty hands,
And now we long for long - lost childhood fields.

Birds carve sorrow in the sky,
Echoes of laughter lost to time.
Once, the rain sang sweet and soft,
Now its song is faint and far.

Take me back to those amber fields,
Where I may rise like the kite.
Take me back to those golden brown fields
Where I am free as the wind.

Miracle Of The Mage

You are the parrot known for breaking a thousand cages,
You are a sonnet with overflowing words on pages
You are the soaring kite in the sky, uncontrolled
by the line
You are the context of my reveries of mine
Vibrant are your colours that even make a
rainbow jealous
Grateful is your creator who did a work so marvellous
Your radiant smile illuminates the soul like a blessing
Your fragrance makes the mood ever refreshing
When you admire the sunset, the sun also blushes
for an instant
I feel the ardent encumbrance towards you
from a distance
Symphonies are sung by the night angels at
your presence
Melodies and lullabies are your bittersweet essence
You are the kite known for breaking a thousand cages,
I wonder if you were created by mages.

When The Beast Is Chained

When the talons rust, when the fangs dull,
When the swift-footed hunter limps, unseen in the tall grass,
And the shadowed beast of the night quivers in the daylight glare
Oh, when the predator feels the bite of its own hunger,
When the hunter gasps beneath the weight of the chase,
Does the moon not still rise? Does the tide not still returning?

Falter not, O weary hands, calloused by the struggle.
For toil is a hymn, and practice is the drumbeat of fate.
Hard work does not die in silence; it carves its echoes in stone.
So what if the fields are barren today?
So what if the winds howl with the voice of despair?
Return, return to the roots of the craft
Move with the patience of rivers carving canyons.
Step again, though the bones groan their protest,
Step again, though the eyelids fall like weary gates.

Rise! Rise from the grave of hesitation!
Seek the pulse of the world, the trembling prey
Study its breath, its heartbeat, its fear.
Sharpen your claws upon the anvil of persistence.
Become not the meek wanderer lost in fate's storm,
But the storm itself, the untamed wind, the unrelenting tide.
For in the quiet march of tireless effort,
The hunter finds his fangs once more.

When Roots Are Uprooted

Move gently through the hush of night,
while we lie still, unaware, in the shelter we once called home.
Did you ever pause to ask,
before you tore down our world brick by brick?
What made you believe this land was ever yours to take?

You shattered what we built to raise your walls of glass,
called it progress, called it vision
A valley of silicon rising where roots once ran deep.
You plant decor in the name of green,
But forests are not things to be arranged.

What becomes of the breath that once rose from Our canopy?
What becomes of our kin, our calls, our quiet lives?
Are we only statistics to be logged and forgotten,
marked endangered, marked obsolete?

To be human is to carry mercy in the bones,
Yet all we meet is steel and thunder.
Will we end up as displays behind bars?
Or memories faded into soil?

We shift from space to space,
But each place shrinks with time,
until nothing remains.

So be gentle in the darkness,
let kindness find its way back.
Remember, we too belong.
Remember, we too are alive.